PEGASUS ENCYCLOPEDIA LIBRARY

Experiments and Activities
NATURE

Edited by: Aparna Chatterji
Managing editor: Tapasi De
Designed by: Vijesh Chahal and Anil Kumar
Illustrated by: Suman S. Roy, Tanoy Choudhury
Colouring done by: Vinay Kumar, Sonu, Kiran Kumari & Pradeep Kumar

NATURE

CONTENTS

Introduction	3
Acid Rain	4
Making an ant farm	6
Tornado in a bottle	8
A home for toads	10
Can evaporation be stopped?	11
Talking to plants makes them grow	12
Growing bacteria	14
Growing plants from seeds	16
Making a pond	17
Rock candy	18
Colour of apple	19
A kitchen garden	20
Make clean water	21
Potatoes that float	22
Make a river	23
Dipping in the pond	24
Layers of soil	25
Your backyard neighbours	26
New plants from old plants	27
Making craters	28
A wavy activity	30
Fossil cast	31
Index	32

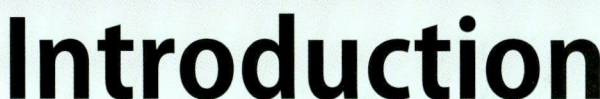

Introduction

Learning and experiencing new things is a continuous process. Children are much more inquisitive than we elders are. They are always bubbling with enthusiasm when it comes to knowing new things. That is the reason they are so full of questions. This enthusiasm should never be curbed; instead, it should be encouraged!

It is a proven fact that children learn the most by doing, experiencing and seeing things. Teaching them through books and worksheets only, does not suffice. We all know that 'seeing is believing'.

But sometimes due to the constraint of time and many other factors, elders are not successful in giving those experiences and exposure to their children which they deserve.

This encyclopedia on Nature is full of activities and experiments related to nature. It will act as a guide, a teacher and help children in increasing their scientific knowledge. Most of the activities and experiments mentioned here can be done by children alone.

This particular encyclopedia will not only teach children many new things about nature but will also make them better citizens as they will become more concerned about their planet Earth!

> **The first Japanese car in the United States was the Honda Accord manufactured in November 1982.**

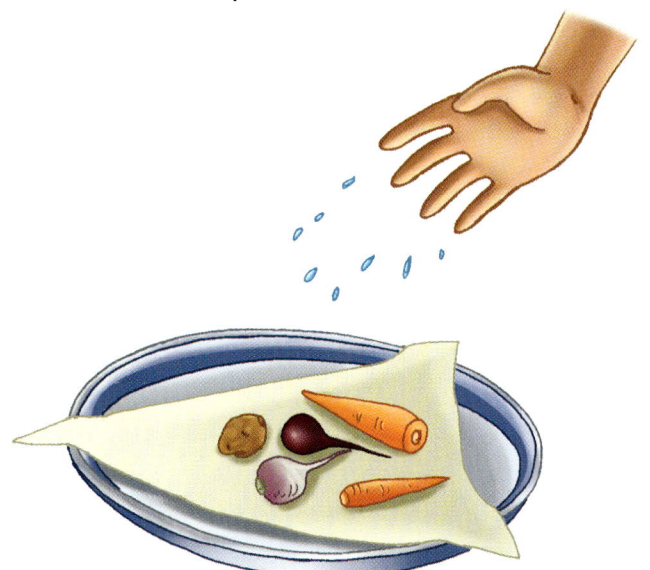

NATURE

Acid Rain

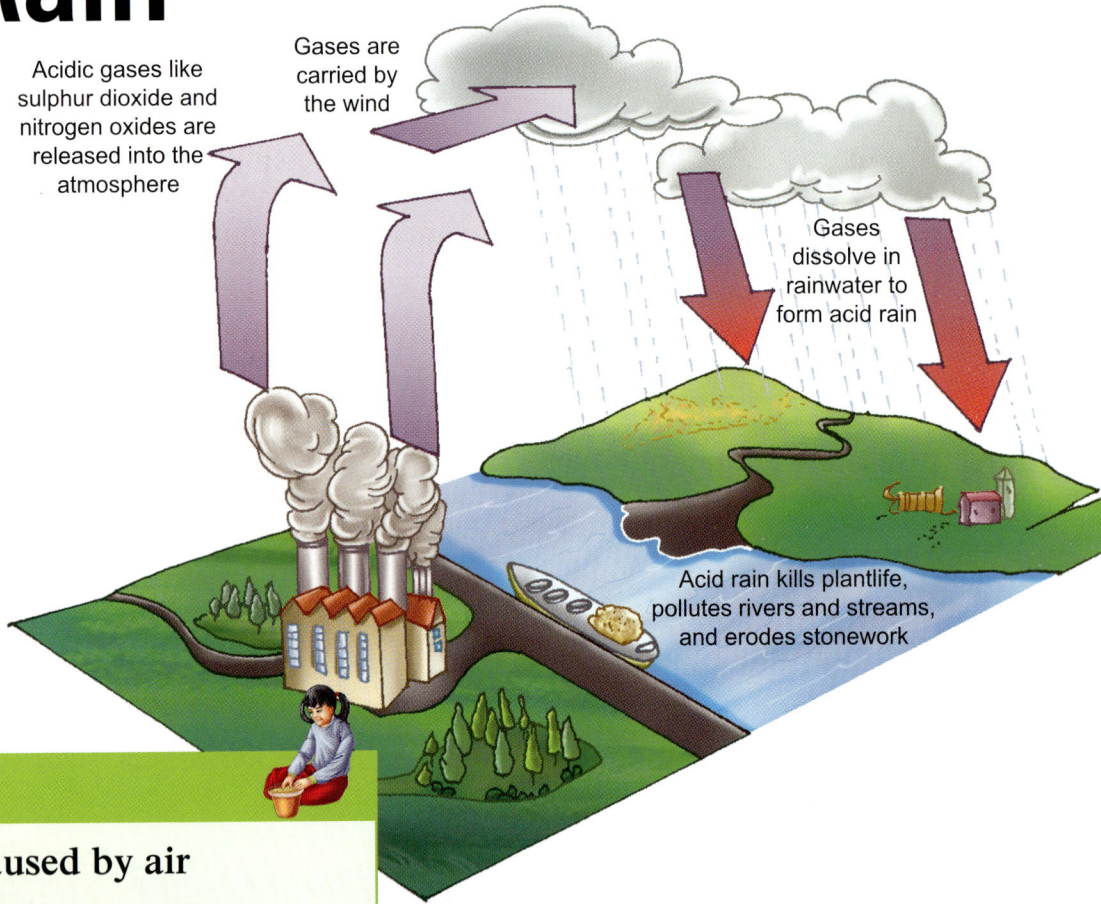

Acidic gases like sulphur dioxide and nitrogen oxides are released into the atmosphere

Gases are carried by the wind

Gases dissolve in rainwater to form acid rain

Acid rain kills plantlife, pollutes rivers and streams, and erodes stonework

The fact

Acid rain is caused by air pollutants in the atmosphere. These pollutants are formed due to the smoke from factories, industries and the exhaust of vehicles. Many other pollutants contribute to acid rain as well. The pollutants gather in dense clouds and fall back to Earth when it rains. The pollutants which are acidic, effect the growth of plant life negatively. Let us see how through this experiment.

What you need

- Three jars with lids
- Three growing bean plants in small cups or small separate planting pots
- Masking tape
- Marking pen
- Lemon juice
- Water
- Tablespoon

How to do the experiment?

1. Label each bean plant container as 'A', 'B', and 'C'.

2. Then, label the three jars with masking tape 'A', 'B', and 'C'.

3. Pour 1/2 cup of lemon juice into jar 'A'.
4. Pour 1/4 cup lemon juice into jar 'B'.
5. Don't put any lemon juice into jar 'C'.
6. Add 1/2 cup of water to each jar (A, B, C).
7. Place the growing bean plants on a windowsill where there is sufficient sunlight.
8. Water each plant with four tablespoons of the solution marked for that particular plant (that is, plant 'A' gets solution 'A', plant 'B' gets solution 'B', plant 'C' gets solution 'C').

What will happen?

Plant 'A' will show the effects of acid rain first. The leaves will begin to curl and shrivel. Its growth will slow down or stop completely. It will begin to look sickly. Next plant 'B' will start to show the effects of acid rain but at a slower pace. Plant 'C' will remain healthy because it received no acid rain at all.

Conclusion

The acid in the lemon juice retards the growth of the plants just like the acids of the acid rain.

NATURE

Making an ant farm

Ants are tiny creatures who are known for their hard working nature and their discipline. Let us learn through this activity how to make an ant farm and have a closer look at the lives of these tiny creatures.

The Ant farm is a very useful and entertaining toy for all ages. One can see the world's tiniest engineers dig tunnels, build roads, erect bridges, and go about their 'chores' around the farmhouse.

What you need

- Ant farm
- A vial full of ants
- Coloured sand meant for the ant farm

How to do the activity?

1. Place the ant farm on a table.
2. Pour the sand into the observation tank. If you have coloured sand, then place it in layers. The ant food is already mixed in the sand.
3. Now wet the sand with a little water. Dampen the whole sand, but don't over do it. You may use a medicine dropper to add the water evenly.
4. Let the wet sand settle for a day or two, keep the lid open to allow excess water to evaporate. The wet sand makes it easier for the ants to dig tunnels.
5. Before putting the ants, you may add some extra food to the sand though it already contains some ant food. You may add things like a small piece of a fruit or a piece of damp bread.
6. Now you may add the ants to complete the farm. But first put the vial containing the ants in the refrigerator for 2-3 minutes. This calms them down while still in the vial. Do not leave them in the freezer for more than 3 minutes. Next, tap the vial with the ants into the farm. Quickly close the lid.

What will happen?

The ants will be busy eating, carrying load and digging tunnels.

Astonishing fact

Did you know that ants are capable of carrying objects 50 times their own body weight with their mandibles.

Making an ant farm

What will you learn?
The ants can be an inspiration to you due to their hard working nature and sense of discipline. You will be surprised how they walk in a perfect queue and how they gather food for odd times!

NATURE

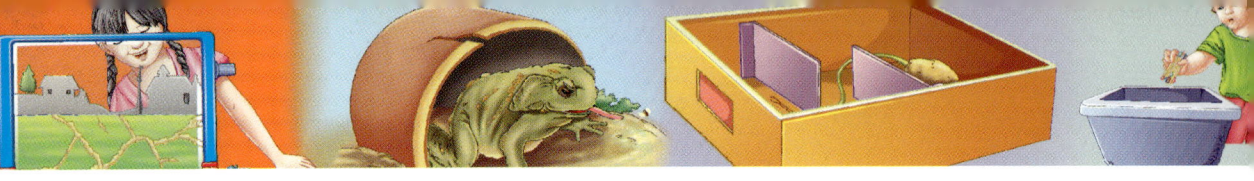

Tornado in a bottle

The fact

A tornado is a violent rotating column of air extending from a thunderstorm to the ground. They are commonly known as twisters. They can cause tremendous destruction by destroying large buildings, uprooting trees and hurling vehicles. Let us see how to make a tornado in a bottle.

What you need

- 2 plastic bottles with capacity of 1 litre each
- Water
- Food colour
- Small styrofoam balls (Optional)
- Small washer 1/4"
- Duct tape

Tornado in a bottle

How to do the activity?

1. Fill one of the empty bottles with water.

2. Add a few drops of food colour to the water.

3. Add the small styrofoam balls also.

4. Put the 1/4 inch washer on top of the filled bottle.

5. Now invert the other bottle on top of it so they are connected. Use the duct tape to make the joint, water tight.

6. Now turn the bottle with the water upside down so that the water is on top and watch how quickly the water gushes to the lower bottle forming a twister.

NATURE

A home for toads

In this fun nature activity, let us make a toad shelter for our friendly backyard neighbours who eat lots of insects.

What you need

- A big, broken ceramic flower pot or bowl
- Mosses and soft leaves

How to do the activity?

1. Turn the broken pot or bowl with the curved side up as a toad shelter. Cover the ground beneath the pot with moist moss and leaves.

2. Make sure you place the pot near an area where there is plenty of water. Then wait for the toads to arrive. After a while, you will notice toads coming and sitting under your pot resting and eating bugs!

What will you learn?

You can observe the behaviour of the toads very closely; that is, which are the insects that the toads generally eat and how they interact with each other.

Can evaporation be stopped?

The fact

We all know that water constantly evaporates from the seas, lakes, rivers and ponds. But it is possible to stop evaporation, which we will show by this experiment.

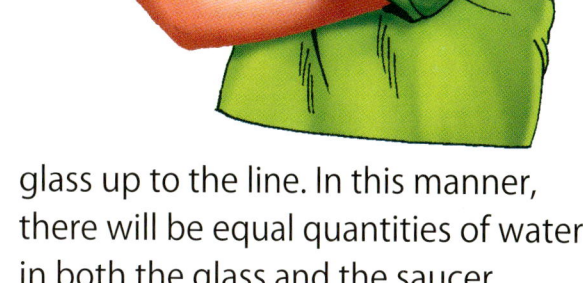

What you need

- A glass
- A saucer
- A marker of any colour

How to do the experiment?

1. Draw a line around half-way up the glass.
2. Fill with water up to the line.
3. Pour the water from the glass into the saucer. Now pour more water into the glass up to the line. In this manner, there will be equal quantities of water in both the glass and the saucer.
4. Cover the glass with another saucer and leave the saucer filled with water, outside.
5. Leave them untouched for a day.

What will happen?

Most of the water in the saucer will have evaporated, while the level of the water in the glass will remain unchanged.

Conclusion

Water evaporates to form water vapour. If this water vapour is carried away by air, then water would continue to evaporate. However, if the water vapour is not carried away by the air, then an equilibrium is reached and there is no further increase in the amount of water vapour formed.

NATURE

Talking to plants makes them grow

The fact

The renowned Indian scientist Jagdish Chandra Bose discovered that plants responded to any kind of stimuli just like animals. His experiments proved that plants grow faster in pleasant music and their growth slows down in noise!

What you need

- 4 small pots of the same size with holes on their bottoms
- Some soil to fill them
- Radish seeds
- Some tap water

How to do the experiment?

1. Fill the pots with soil.
2. Moisten the soil with little tap water
3. Sprinkle 8-10 ordinary radish seeds on the soil.
4. Now sprinkle about 1/4 inch of soil over the seeds and put water again. Be careful not to water it too much.
5. Water them lightly every day.
6. After the seeds sprout, place all the pots together, preferably outdoors where there is ample sunlight.
7. Label each pot with a name or number.

Indian Scientist Jagdish Chandra Bose

Talking to plants makes them grow

How will you treat the plants?

1. Ignore one pot of plants. Never pick it up or give it any attention.
2. Say 'hello', smile and say a few nice words every day to the second plant for about 15 seconds.
3. Behave similarly with the third plant also, but spend about 1 minute speaking soft and nice words of affection. The child should also gently touch the leaves.
4. Treat the fourth plant very kindly. Fawn over the plant in words and gestures. Gently stroke the leaves and speak with much affection. Spend as much time per leaf as you can. Each session should be of 2 minutes.

What will happen?

Generally, radishes mature in 35-45 days. When you review the plants after this period you will see that all the 4 plants have different growth levels. You may note the differences in plant size, leaf colour and taste. The plants to whom you have shown affection will surely show higher growth rate than the others.

Conclusion

Plants do respond better when they are talked to and when affection is shown, just like animals.

NATURE

Growing bacteria

The fact

Bacteria are a fascinating type of microorganism that play quite an important role in our lives. Let us grow our own sample of bacteria and see how it reproduces in a short span of time.

What you need

- Petrie dish of agar
- Cotton buds
- Some old newspaper

How to do the experiment?

1. Prepare your petrie dish of agar.
2. Using your cotton buds, swab any area of your house that is, collect a sample by rubbing the cotton bud on a surface of your choice (like kitchen sink or bathroom wash basin).
3. Rub the swab over the agar with a few gentle zig zag strokes before putting the lid back on the petrie dish.
4. Keep the dish in a warm area for 2 or 3 days.
5. Check the growth of bacteria each day by making an observational drawing and describing the changes.
6. Dispose off the bacteria by wrapping up the petrie dish in an old newspaper and placing it in the dustbin.

Growing bacteria

Warning

Do not open the lid while throwing.

Note: A Petri dish is a shallow glass or plastic lidded dish that scientists use to culture cells or small mosses. It was named after the German bacteriologist Julius Richard Petri, who invented it.

What will happen?

The agar plate and warm conditions provided the ideal conditions for the bacteria to grow. The bacteria on the plate grow into colonies, each a clone of the original. They steadily grow and become visible to the naked eye in a relatively short time. Different samples produce different results. You will find bacteria throughout the Earth; it grows in soil, radioactive waste, water, on plants and even animals too.

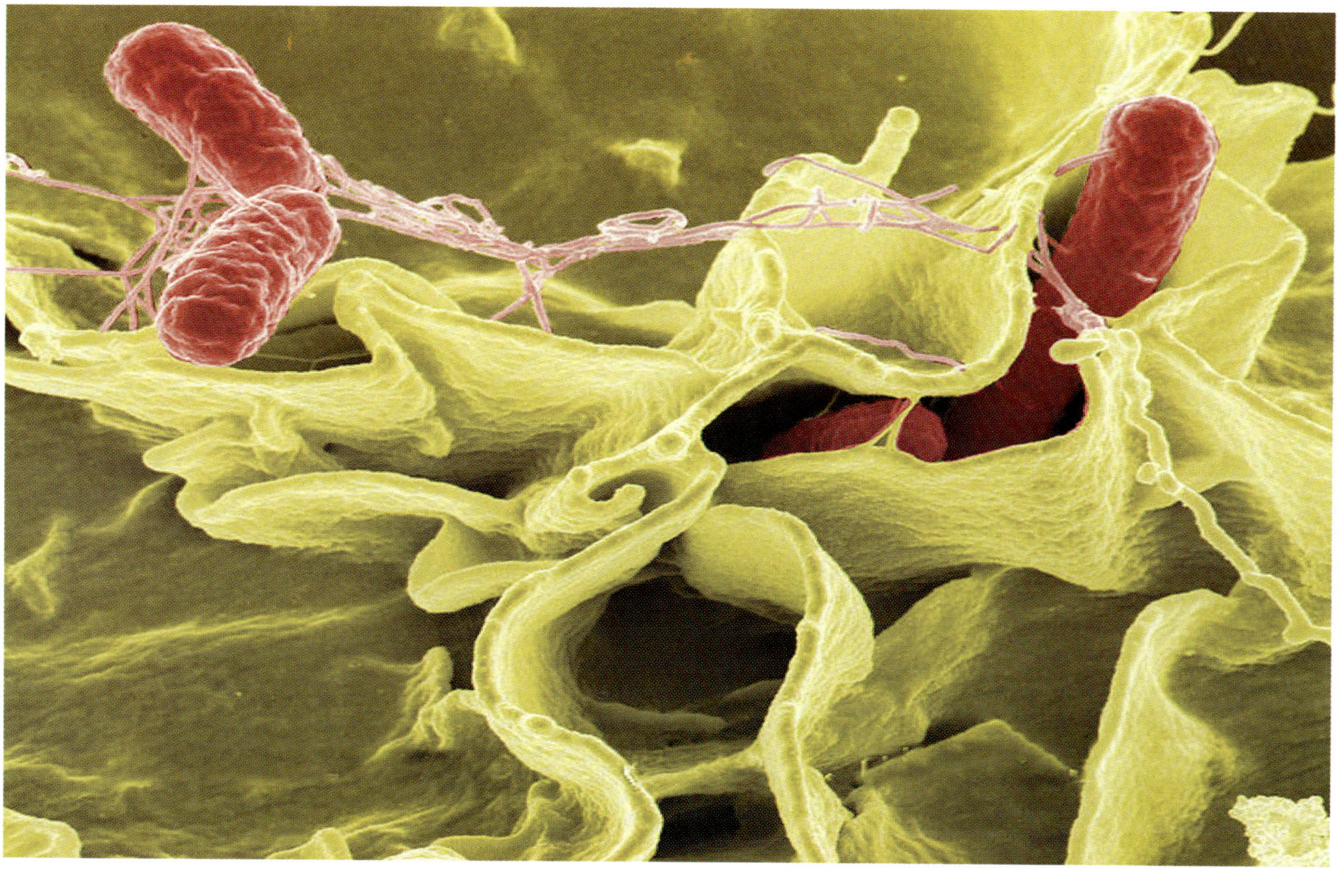

A step further

Try repeating the process with a new petrie dish and swab from under your finger nails or between your toes.

15

NATURE

Growing plants from seeds

The fact

When given the right temperature, sunlight and water, seeds grow into young seedlings. Let us grow our own seedling and monitor its growth though this experiment.

What you need

- Pumpkins seeds or sunflower seeds
- Good quality soil (you can also buy some potting soil from your local garden store)
- A pot to hold the soil and your seeds
- Water
- sunlight

How to do the experiment?

1. Fill the pot with soil.
2. Plant the seeds inside the soil.
3. Place the pot in some place where there is sunlight though try to avoid too much direct sunlight; a window sill is a good place for this.
4. Keep the soil moist by watering it everyday but do not water it too much.
5. Record your observations.

What will happen?

After a week of care, the seeds will germinate and tiny seedlings will sprout.

Making a pond

A pond is body of water smaller than a lake. Let us make a pond by ourselves and see how many animals we can attract to it.

What you need

- A flat tray
- Gravel
- Soil
- Large stones
- Some water plants such as pond weed

How to do the activity?

1. Cover the tray with gravel and some soil. Put a big stone in the middle to make an island.
2. Now fill the tray with rain water as it is best for a pond.
3. Place the plants fixing them with stones and soil.
4. Make a chart of your pond. Note which animals visit your pond and where they stay. Make comparisons from day to day.

Visitors you may have

Mosquito

Turtle

Snails

Frogs

Dragon flies

NATURE

Rock candy

We all love to eat candies, don't we? Let's make one at home! It only requires a few simple ingredients and just a little time and patience.

What you need

- 15cm piece of string
- A pencil
- A paper clip (or large plastic bead)
- 1 cup of water
- 2 cups of sugar
- A glass jar

How to do the experiment?

1. Tie the 15cm piece of string to the middle of the pencil.
2. Tie the paper clip (or bead) onto the end of the string.
3. Put the pencil across the top of a jar so that the string hangs down into the middle of the jar.
4. If it hangs down too far into the jar, roll the string around the pencil until the string withdraws a little. The string should not touch the sides or bottom of the jar. The string with the bead or the paper clip will act as a seed for the crystal.
5. Now the string and the pencil are ready. Remove them from the jar and put them aside.
6. Pour water into a pan and bring it to boil. Pour about 1/4 cup of sugar into the boiling water; stir it until it dissolves.
7. Keep adding more and more sugar, each time stirring it until it dissolves, until no more will dissolve. Such a solution is called a saturated solution.
8. Carefully pour the hot sugar solution into the jar. Then submerge the paper clip or bead tied to the string into the sugar solution. Be sure the string hangs down into the sugar solution.
9. Allow the contents of the jar to cool and put it in someplace where it will not be moved and shaken. In about a week you will have a large crystals to lick!

Colour of apple

The fact

When sliced apple pieces are kept exposed, they turn brown. Then we do not feel like eating them. But we can prevent this very easily. Let us perform this simple experiment and find out how.

What you need

- An apple
- Half a lemon
- Shallow bowl
- Water
- Knife

How to do the experiment?

1. Peel and slice an apple.
2. Place one slice in a shallow bowl full of water.
3. Smear the second slice with the juice of half a lemon.
4. Leave the third slice exposed to air.
5. Wait for an hour; then compare.

What will happen?

The slice with nothing on it turns brown.

Conclusion

When an apple is cut open, chemicals inside the apple combine with oxygen from the air to form a brown coating. The coating keeps coming in contact with oxygen which goes deeper into the apple slice. Water prevents the first slice from oxygen in the air; so it remains white. Vitamin C in the lemon juice, contains antioxidents which keep oxygen away from the second slice. So, it stays white for the longest time.

NATURE

A kitchen garden

The fact

Learning about how plants grow can be simple and interesting. You may observe this process of growing a plant without soiling your hands with mud through a simple activity on your mom's kitchen table! Let us see how.

What you need

- Root vegetables like carrots, parsnips, turnips, beets, potatoes
- Knife and cutting board
- Paper towels
- Shallow dish or plate
- Water

How to do the experiment?

1. Chop the top parts of each vegetable (about 1 inch thick)
2. Place 2 sheets of paper towels on a plate or shallow dish. Wet the sheets with water.
3. Place the vegetable tops on the moist sheets of paper towels.
4. Leave the dish beside a window from where sunlight filters in.
5. Check the paper towel daily to see if its moist and add freshwater when the paper towels start getting dry.

What will happen?

A few days later, the vegetables will sprout looking like a small garden.

Make 'clean water'

Most of us do not think much about the cleanliness of water that we use. This is because we are all used to clean water in our daily lives so naturally we seldom care to think about it. Let us see how you can get clean and pure water through the experiment given below.

What you need

- Gravel
- Sand
- Blotting paper or 3 or 4 coffee filters
- A clean flower pot
- Transparent jug
- Large measuring cup or pouring jug

How to do the experiment?

1. Place blotting paper, sand and finally gravel in a clean flower pot.
2. Place the flower pot in a larger transparent vessel so the filtered water can drip through the hole and the children can see it.
3. In a big measuring cup, put some dirt, bits of plants, leaves and water.
4. Mix it well to make muddy water.
5. Pour the muddy water into the flower pot as shown in the image.

What will happen?

The water will drip from the flower pot and gather into the transparent vessel. This water will be cleaner and clearer.

Conclusion

The layers of sand, gravel and blotting paper act as filters holding back the dirt and helping in filtering the water.

A step further

You may arrange the layers in a different order and compare the colour of the filtered water.

NATURE

Potatoes that float

The fact

It is seen that objects generally float in liquids with higher density than plain water. Let us see this through a simple experiment.

What you need

- Three potato slices
- Three glasses of water
- A spoon
- Salt or sugar

How to do the experiment?

1. Make a concentrated solution of salt or sugar in a glass of water. Number the glass as 1.
2. In the second glass, create a layered mix of sugar or salt water with regular water on top of it. To create a layered mix, pour concentrated sugar syrup into the second glass till it is half filled and then top it up with regular water.
3. Leave the water in the third glass alone.
4. Place potato slices in each glass.

What will happen?

- The slice that is dropped into the first glass will float in the salt solution.
- The potato slice put in the second glass will sink halfway and float in the middle of the glass.
- The last slice will sink to the bottom of the glass.

Conclusion

The first glass had a saturated solution of salt or sugar which was denser than the potato slice. So, the slice floated. The density of the second solution was a little more than the second slice. So the second slice floated in the middle of the glass. But the density of water was less than the potato slice in the third glass. In other words, the potato slice was heavier than the water. So it sank to the bottom of the glass.

Make a river

Rivers are one of the richest and the most fertile sources of water on the surface of the Earth. They are formed when water from rain, melted snow, lakes and springs collects together shaping its way through the Earth. Let us make a mini river and see it meandering.

What you need

- Small stones
- Some soil
- A metal or plastic tray
- A jug of water

How to do the activity?

1. Cover the tray with mud.
2. Place the stones in one corner of the tray.
3. Cover the stones with soil. Shape it in such a manner so that it looks like a hill.
4. Now put some stones on the sides of the hill on top of the soil.
5. Fill the jug with water and pour it on the top of the hill.

What will happen?

The mini river will move forward, down the hill making channels and carrying soil downhill.

What did you learn?

This activity demonstrated the movement of a river and how it carries soil with it.

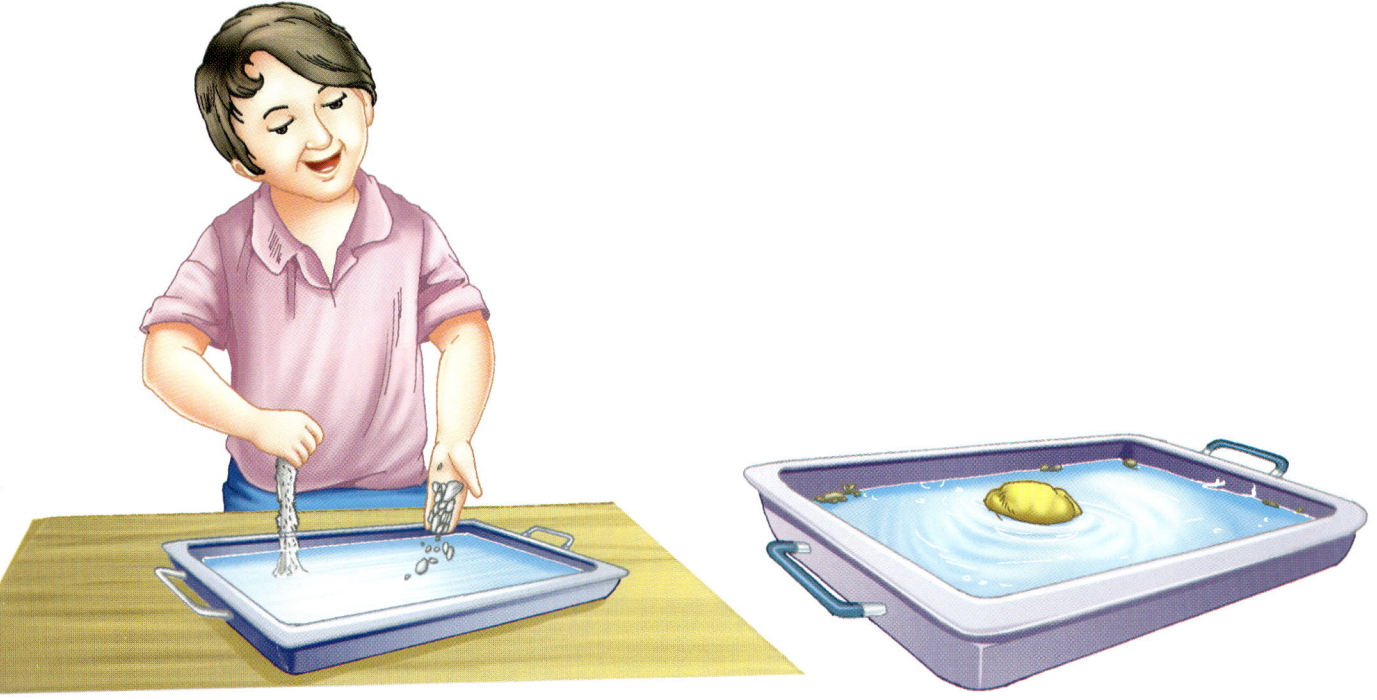

Dipping in the pond

Ponds are water bodies smaller than lakes. Spring and summers are considered to be the best time to go for pond dipping with plastic containers. You will find all kinds of plants and animals living in the pond.

What you need

- A plastic container
- A fine net
- A magnifying glass

How to do the activity?

1. Fill your plastic container with pond water. The container should be cleaned properly before use.
2. Sweep your net in the water of the pond.
3. Empty the contents of the net into another container.
4. With a magnifying glass, examine all the plants and creatures you have caught.
5. Now sweep your net in the middle of the pond. What did you find?

What you may find in the pond

- Sticklebacks
- Great pond snails
- Leeches
- Water boatman
- Mosquitoes

Layers of soil

Soil is an important part of our Earth. It is generally full of minerals and water that plants need for growth. Many tiny creatures like moles and worms also make it their home.

What you need

- Some soil
- A bucket
- A sieve
- A screw-top jar

How to do the activity?

1. Dig up some soil from your backyard and put it in a bucket.

2. Sieve some soil with the help of a sieve onto some paper and see what is left behind. You may find stones, bits of plants or even tiny living creatures in the soil.

3. Now put some soil into a screw-top jar. Fill the jar almost to the top with water and screw on the lid tightly.

4. Shake the jar vigorously until all the contents mix properly; then leave the jar for sometime.

5. After a while, look at the jar carefully. The soil will settle into layers in the water.

NATURE

Your backyard neighbours

There are many small creatures such as spiders, snails, millipedes and slugs that stay in your backyard. Seldom do we think about them. Many a time, we are even scared of them. But did you know that these tiny creatures form a very vital part of our environment? Let us set a trap and try to attract a few of these through this activity.

How to do the activity?

Preparing the trap

1. Dig a hole in the soil deep enough to hold a small container. Fill it with pieces of fruits and a spoonful of cat food and dog food.

2. Cover the hole (trap) with a small stone propped up at one end with another stone so that there is a small gap.

3. Leave the trap overnight. Lift the rock to see what you have caught. Before you let your tiny neighbours leave, try to find out what they are.

New plants from old plants

Plants are generally grown from seeds. But some plants can be grown from old plants without using seeds! A potato is a starchy plant tuber that is packed with food that a new potato plant needs to grow. It has little buds on its surface called eyes. Let us grow new potato plants with the help of old ones through this activity.

What you need

- A potato with eyes or buds
- A shoe box with a lid
- Cardboard
- Scissors
- Tape

How to do the activity?

1. Bend the end of each strip of cardboard to make a flap. Tape the flaps to the sides of the box to make a maze.
2. Place the potato in the box and put on the lid. After a few days, shoots will start to grow from the eyes through the maze towards the light.

What will happen?

A potato plant will grow from a piece of a potato bulb.

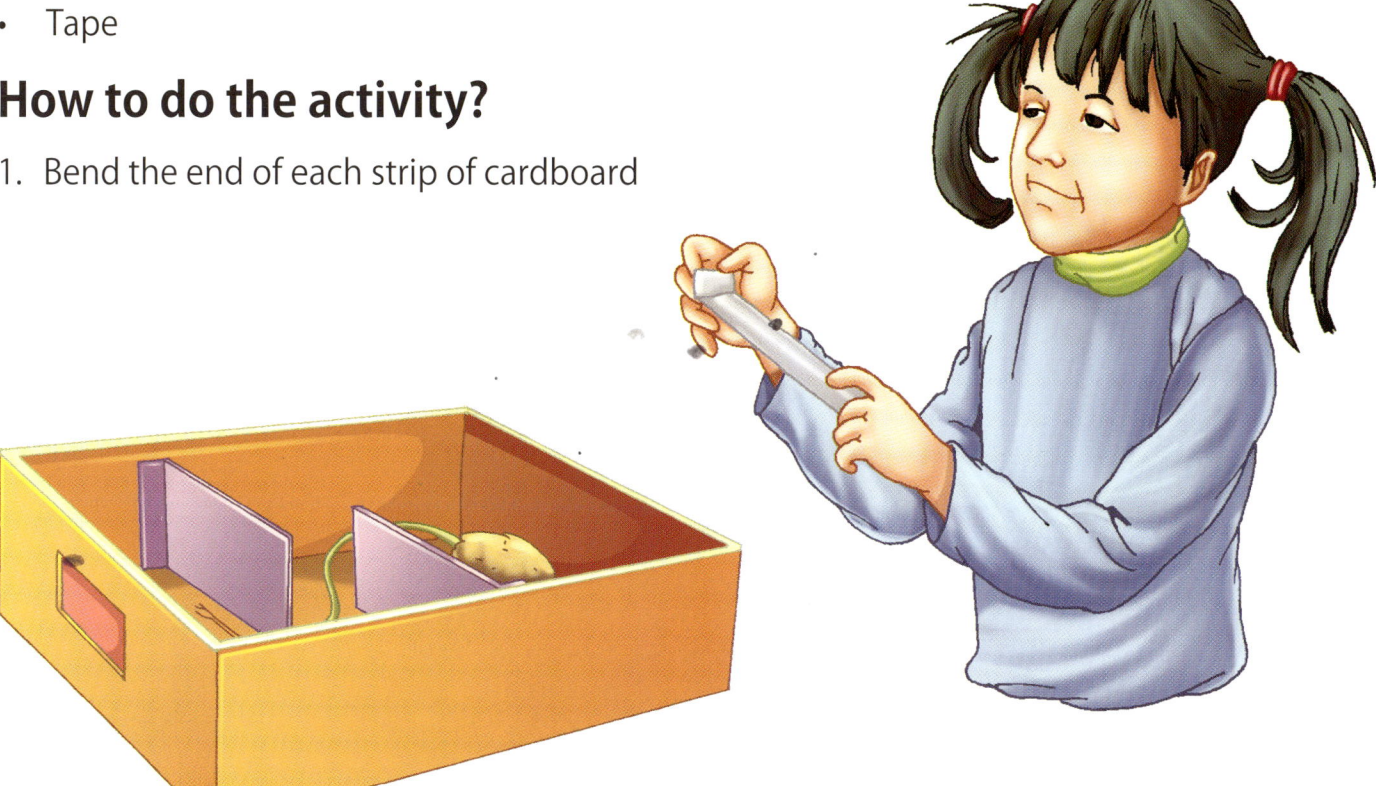

Making craters

Meteors, and comets are heavenly bodies which sometimes hurl at great speeds and collide with the surface of the Earth. It is then that they form holes or craters on the Earth's surface. Let us make such craters and see what are the factors that affect the size and depth of such craters.

What you need

- Flour (or sand or soil)
- 1 cup hot chocolate powder or cocoa
- A big, deep container
- Ruler
- Small, medium and large marbles or rocks, ping pong or golf balls
- A string of 1.5 metres
- Drop cloth, newspaper or any other floor covering

How to do the experiment?

1. Spread the drop cloth or newspaper or try this outside as this experiment maybe a little messy.

2. Place the container in the middle of the drop cloth and fill the tray three inches high with flour (or sand or soil). Make sure the flour is spread evenly across the pan.

3. Now, sprinkle a thin, even layer of hot chocolate powder on top.

4. Now sit close to the tray. Gather the impactors (marbles or rocks), string and ruler.

5. Make craters in the following way

    - Mark the string at 30 cm and again at 1.5m.

    - Roughly calculate the diameter of each of your impactors using a ruler.

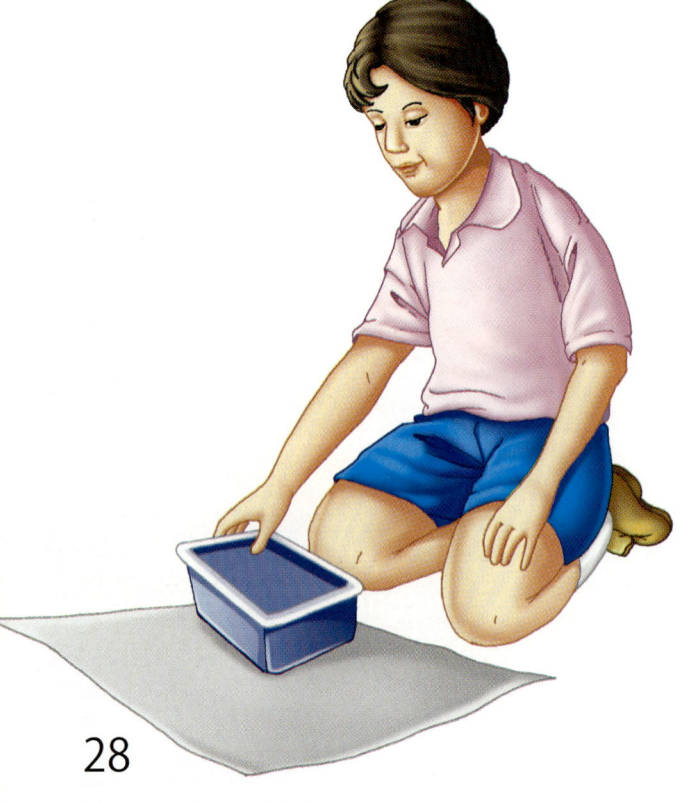

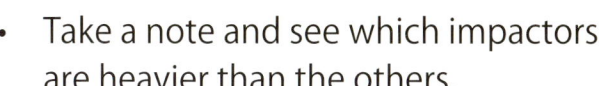

- Take a note and see which impactors are heavier than the others.
- Drop the first impactor from a height of 30 cm.
- Measure the diameter and depth of the crater it forms. Record your findings.
- Drop the first impactor again from a height of 1.5 m. Be sure to drop it away from your first crater. Record your findings.
- Repeat these steps with the other impactors.

What will happen?

Different impactors will form craters of different sizes and depths.

What did you learn?

When comets and asteroids collide with planets, they create impact craters. The size and depth of impact craters increase with the size, speed and travelling distance of these heavenly bodies. The bigger the object and the faster it travels, the bigger the crater. This is because bigger and faster meteors release more energy when they collide with another body.

NATURE

A wavy activity

Let us find out how liquids of different densities interact and let us form wavy patterns with this experiment.

What you need

- Clear plastic bottle with a tight cap
- Water
- Food colour
- Mineral oil

How to do the activity?

1. Fill half the plastic bottle with water.
2. Add blue or green food colour until the water gets dark.
3. Now add mineral oil until the container overflows just a little.
4. Close the cap tightly on.
5. Now tilt the bottle on its side, rock it gently and watch the waves that form. Keep the bottle rocking and continue observing the wavy patterns. Can you make the waves 'collide'?

What will happen?

When the bottle is static, you will see that the oil stands on top of the water. This happens because oil is less dense than water. As you rock the bottle, you will see the wavy patterns. If you rock the bottle with varying force you will create different patterns of waves.

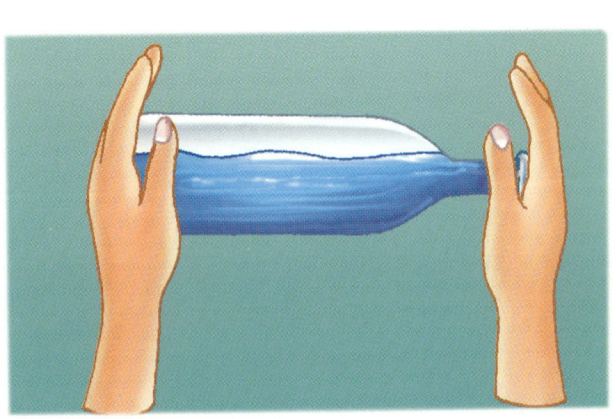

30

Fossil cast

Fossils are not only interesting records of the past, but they are also beautiful to look at. In this activity you can make a fossil mold or cast in just a few hours. Your fossil cast will have the same details and delicate patterns that a real fossil has.

What you need

- A chunk of plasticine clay (about the size of your fist)
- Dull table knife
- 2 paper cups; bottom should be 25 to 6 cm in diameter
- A sea shell or a small bone
- About 1/2 cup of plastic of Paris
- 1/4 cup of water
- Spoon

How to do the activity?

1. Take a half of clay and flatten it until its about 2.5cm thick and smooth at the top. Trim the circle of the clay until it fits the bottom of the cup.

2. Slide the clay into the cup, flat side up. Carefully press the shell or bone into the clay. Then carefully lift the object out of the clay. You will be able to see an impression of the object.

3. Pour the plaster of Paris into the other cup. Add water and stir til the mixture is smooth.

4. After two to three mixtures pour the mixture into the other paper cup right on top of the clay. Let it sit for on hour without touching it.

5. After an hour, carefully tear away the sides of the paper cup and remove the clay and plaster. Holding the clay part in one hand and the plaster part with the other hard, gently separate them.

6. Use the knife to carefully trim away any rough edges from the plaster fossil cast. Smooth out the edges, the let it dry for a day or two. Your fossil print is now ready.

Index

A
acid rain 4, 5
agar 14, 15
atmosphere 4

B
bacteria 14
blotting paper 21

C
channels 23
comets 28, 29
craters 28, 29
crystal 18

D
density 22

G
germinate 16
gravel 17, 21

M
magnifying glass 24
meteors 28, 29
microorganism 14

P
parsnips 20

Petrie dish 14, 15
pollutants 4

R
radioactive 15
reproduces 14

S
sprout 12, 16, 20
Sticklebacks 24
stimuli 12
styrofoam 8, 9
submerge 18

T
temperature 16
tornado 8
transparent 21

W
Water boatman 24